# GOING UP AND COMING DOWN FROM DRUGS AND ALCOHOL

## BY KENNETH MICHAEL SPALDING

iUniverse, Inc.
New York   Bloomington

iUniverse books may be ordered through booksellers or by contacting:

iUniverse
1663 Liberty Drive
Bloomington, IN 47403
www.iuniverse.com
1-800-Authors (1-800-288-4677)

Because of the dynamic nature of the Internet, any Web addresses or links contained in this book may have changed since publication and may no longer be valid. The views expressed in this work are solely those of the author and do not necessarily reflect the views of the publisher, and the publisher hereby disclaims any responsibility for them.

ISBN: 978-1-4401-4611-4 (sc)
ISBN: 978-1-4401-4610-7 (ebook)

Printed in the United States of America

iUniverse rev. date: 7/8/2009

**To my friend Martha**
**My companion on the search for peace and**
**tranquility ...**

# Contents

# PREFACE

I am writing this book because if I didn't stop living the way that I was living I would die.

I had a normal childhood, but I still turned to a life of substance abuse. I don't know if I turned to using drugs and alcohol because of insecurities from my low self esteem, or because of my homosexuality.

I went from drinking alcohol, to smoking marijuana, to popping pills, to taking L.S.D, to injecting heroin, and to taking anything that was put in front of me. I spent a lot of years where my main purpose in life was to satisfy my cravings.

Life is too short. And physical complications do come from abusing drugs and alcohol. I've had a vein burst in my esophagus, and I almost bled to death. My stomach was pumped several times, and I suffered horrible DT's (delirium tremors). I have Hepatitis C, a serious virus of the blood, and I also may need to have a liver transplant.

Just to have survived the massive amounts of drugs that I would take and the large amounts of alcohol that I would drink is a miracle. I am very lucky to be able to write this book. This is how I remember my story.

# I
# Stage One Of My Life

*My childhood years in Alabama*

My journey started on January 16, 1962 in Haleyville, Alabama. I was born the youngest of four brothers. The second to the oldest brother died of meningitis before I was born. I don't have any remembrance of him. I really don't remember much before the age of five. I do have some memories of when I was smaller, but those memories just pop into my sub consciousness at will.

My family had moved from Bardwell, Kentucky to Haleyville, Alabama prior to my birth, in the late fifties or early sixties. It was a small southern town of about ten thousand people. The stores in the downtown area gave you that quaint feeling of being in a small town, because they rolled up the sidewalks at five and because the stores were like the small stores in Bardwell, but it was a bigger city than what my family was used to. I guess that is the charm that attracted my father there in the first place.

My mom was from Illinois and my dad was from Kentucky; when they married they settled in the town where my dad was from.

They were not rich, but my dad did okay at supporting a family. He worked for Illinois Central Gulf Railroad. He knew a little bit about everything, so he had many hobbies. He was the bread winner of the family, while my mom was a stay-at-home mom.

It was unusual for a woman to have a job at that time. It was the sixties and if she did have a job it was probably selling Tupperware or Avon. But over all we had a good life.

My family was pretty normal, but we were no "Norman Rockwell" family. The time of June and Ward Clever with Wally and the Beaver had ended in the fifties. We lived out in the suburbs in a nice house. "Everyone had to keep up with the Joneses." To have the status symbol of being middle class seemed to mean that you had to have the newest or the most expensive car on the block, or a boat, or some other kind of expensive item that would be noticed when someone drove by, sitting in your perfectly manicured lawn. All of the houses along the street had a new car parked in the driveway, and we were no exception; ours was dark red.

We grew up doing the normal things brothers do. Each day we couldn't wait for the latest episode of Dark Shadows to come on. On the weekends my brothers would let me stay up late, until the TV would sign off at midnight and play the Star Spangled Banner. After the television was turned off we would watch the spot of light on the tube get smaller and smaller until it would disappear. I could be entertained by the simplest things.

One of our favorite things to do was to go exploring underneath our house. I still remember how pitch black it would be after crawling into one of the vents from the outside where it was sunny, into the dark and the moldy smelling basement. It was fun crawling along underneath the house until I would crawl into a spider web! I have a fear of spiders to this day; maybe I developed my phobia of spiders from crawling around the basement when I was a little boy.

When the winds would start to blow in March we would like to fly kites. My kite was the kind that was made of paper attached to balsa wood sticks that made up the frame; it was triangular in shape and you had to tie a cloth on the end of it to make the tail. I would run, unwinding the string until the kite had enough length in the string to become air borne. It would go so high that it would look like a little bird, instead of the big kite it was. It would stay airborne for a little while and then it would come soaring back to earth. I would keep doing that over and over again, until I tired myself out. That is what we would do in the spring. Then the summer months would come. It would be so hot that I wouldn't feel like doing anything. The fall months would come and we would start playing outside again. Then my favorite time of year would come, the winter months.

We would have fun when we would go hiking in the woods after an ice storm. Everything would be covered in ice and snow, and would glisten when the sun came out from behind a cloud and cast its rays on it. It would feel so good to be in the crisp cold air of winter. Haleyville seemed like a mystical place. I had so much fun when I was little! Even the aluminum Christmas tree with the rotating light in front of it seemed magical. For the first six years of my life I lived in that place called Haleyville, then my family moved back to Bardwell, Kentucky.

# Stage Two Of My Life

### *My childhood years in Kentucky*

We moved back to Bardwell in 1969. Since my father was a fair man, he let us kids help pick out the house that we would move into. I guess he wanted us to feel like we had a say-so in the decision of the move. I wanted to move into an old, scary haunted looking house.

My father did decide on an old house on the highway near downtown Bardwell; he remodeled it, but it still had that haunted house feeling about it.

The move to Bardwell was a good thing for me; I got to be close to my father's family, and I would get to play with my cousins with whom I had a special bond.

My cousins and I would keep ourselves busy; we always could

find things to do. We used to spend hours digging in the dirt looking for lucky rocks or we would play in the grassy fields looking for four leaf clovers for good luck.

Other than the simple stuff we would do to keep ourselves busy there was not a lot to do in Bardwell. It was the seventies so I spent a lot of time watching what I assumed were acid influenced kid's shows on television like H.R Puffinstuff, Sigmund and the Sea monster and Lids Ville and stuff. I enjoyed these shows and I dreamed that the Slestak monsters from The Land of the Lost were going to come and get me, so in my dreams I would have to find a pylon to hide in.

After school or in the summer months, one of my favorite places to play was the old Bardwell School. We would go to the playground and play tag, red rover, or the childhood games that young people played. The smell of the freshly cut grass from the grounds of the school would bring back some kind of déjà vu memories from when I was a small child. I get those memories to this day when ever someone is cutting the grass in a nearby yard or field.

Afterwards we would go home and the sky would be filled with twinkling lights as fire flies filled the summer sky. They would fill the horizon with little points of light. I would catch the fire flies and put them into a jar, hoping that the grass that I had put in there would be enough food to keep them alive, and that the holes that I had poked in the lid were big enough to let oxygen in for the bugs to breath. I would watch the bugs through the glass as they lit up their tails, until finally I would get bored, and let the fire flies go.

During the winter months, after I had moved back to Bardwell, after a big snow, we would set in front of the television set full of anticipation with our fingers crossed hoping that our school would be one of the schools announced that would be closed. After hearing the joyous news that our school would be closed we would bundle up in our coats, gloves, and scarf's to go sledding down Harlan's Hill (one of the biggest and best hills to slide down in Bardwell). Then after we got cold we would go inside to warm ourselves in front of the old Warm Morning heater. After we would get warm we would get bundled up and go out into the cold to play again.

# II
# Stage Three Of My Life

*My middle school years*

I had gone through my grade school years of having fun and now I was in my middle school years. It was a time of confusion. I was excited about going into the seventh grade, but I was scared as well. I didn't have a lot of friends so I spent most of my days reading tabloids, watching movies on television, playing with my toys or riding my spider bike which had a sissy bar and a banana seat. I remember going to the local gas station to ride my bike over the bell hose to hear the ding come from the back room. I would do that over and over again until the attendant would come out and chase me off.

When I did start seventh grade, I was still the little boy that wanted to play. But I did go to school each day, and since I didn't have a lot of friends, I focused my time on my studies. The teachers really liked me because I showed an interest in learning. If they only had known that the reason I studied so much was because I didn't have anything else to do, they would have thought much differently.

During those years I spent a lot of time with my mom. I always waited in anticipation for Saturday to come because that was the day my mom would do her grocery shopping. I looked forward to going with Mom so I could get the latest edition of the celebrity magazines; I loved to read stories about the stars of then present times and also about stars of yesterday.

I thought that what I was doing was exciting, but I was starting to get older and I was beginning to grow out of the juvenile stuff that I thought of as fun. I was getting too old to be enjoying the trip to get groceries with my mom, or at least I thought I was. I would be starting high school in one year. My childhood innocence was over.

I wasn't supposed to enjoy the activities that I enjoyed when I was young, now I was supposed to enjoy the activities that you normally enjoy when you grow older. The times of watching cartoons and playing childish games were ending. I would be going from my middle school years to my high school years, and it was time for me to grow up.

# Stage Four Of My Life

### *My high school years*

When I started high school, I really felt out of place. In high school everyone was dating people of the opposite sex. I had already gone through puberty, but I felt different. I had a feeling that I knew was not normal. I felt like I wanted to be close to a person of the same sex. As other males were attracted to other females, here I was feeling attracted to other men. I don't know when I realized that I was different, I think I had known in the back of my mind that I felt differently since the time I was a child in Alabama.

I had always enjoyed hanging around with girls, but for different reason than most boys would. Girls were not as intimidating as guys were; not only did I like their personalities, but other people would assume that I was dating them.

I tried to like girls, but I just didn't. I liked to be around them, but sexually I wanted to be close to a man. It was very confusing to have those kinds of feelings. It was something that I would have to figure out and find a way to live with the way that I felt.

# Stage Five Of My Life

### My drug experiment starts

At this time, everyone else was experimenting with drugs. Even after seeing Robbie Benson in *Reds*, (a movie about a boy addicted to pills), and seeing *Scared Straight* (a movie about what could happen if you were sent to prison), I also decided to experiment with drugs.

I started to experiment with different substances. I also began to drink until I got drunk. The alcohol and drug use helped me block out the thoughts of having to deal with the fact that I felt attracted to other men. And they made me feel at ease when I was around my peers.

It was the time right after everyone was turning on, tuning in, and dropping out. It was the generation where anything went. Drugs were what everyone I knew was doing and they provided a perfect escape.

I let my hair grow long, and I dressed in the same type of clothes as the people with whom I hung around dressed in. At this time, the fashion was bell bottom jeans and a T-shirt. It was right after the decade of the flower children; everyone wanted to look like a hippie, and act like one too. And I was willing to try anything.

The first drug that everyone tried was marijuana. I don't know why, I guess it seemed less harmful than the other harder drugs. I was scared but I tried it. I inhaled the smoke from the joint that was passed to me. I didn't want to be called a "narc," so I took a big hit. But the first time I tried smoking marijuana it had no effect on me; or if it did, I did not realize it. After the first time, every time I would smoke it, I got really high.   When I smoked marijuana I experienced everything from non stop laughing fits, to eating any kind of food that was put in front of me to being very thirsty. When I was high, music sounded much better loud. And for some reason music made more sense after I had indulged in the high that marijuana gave me.

Almost every time after I smoked it, the effects would be good; but sometimes it would make me feel very insecure and very shy and would make me realize my true feelings of being gay. I didn't like realizing my true feelings, and I hated the feelings of being insecure; but I didn't always get those feelings so I was willing to take my chances and hope to have a good experience. The best way for me to describe a good pot experience is when, after smoking it, everything seemed animated. The sky would look as if it had been colored blue with a bright blue crayon, the trees and grass looked as if colored with a bright green crayon, and the road would seem blacker than ever, with a bright yellow stripe leading to a magical land.

I would smoke marijuana in anything that would make the high more intense. I've used a device called a power hitter (which I know a lot of people won't even know what it is), a device called a water bong, which was another device that was popular in the seventies, and a Frisbee that was made to hold a joint. I have tried almost everything that was made for smoking marijuana. I liked the feeling I got from marijuana, but I was also willing to try any chemical.

I was offered a Valium, a minor tranquilizer, so I took it and I felt my stressful feelings float away. I would not be embarrassed, and I would not feel that awkward feeling I would get when I was talking to someone. When I think back, it is probably one of the feelings I liked the most; not only did it make me feel less awkward, but it also masked the homosexual feelings I was having. It's hard to imagine that a little pill could do so much, but like they say "dynamite comes in small packages"; well, so do tranquilizers!

During this time I also started to experiment with a pill called Quaalude. It was a pill prescribed for sleep. Back then Rorer made them; then they were made by a company called Lemmon, and then they were outlawed and you could only get bootleg "ludes." I spent a lot of my years luded out. Even when I moved to Miami in 1982, if I was lucky enough to find some real good fake Quaaludes, I would take them. Years later, people would come up to me and say "I remember you and Denise (my future wife) crawling down the sidewalks of Coconut Grove trying to get home." We would be so luded out that we couldn't stand up. Sometimes we would both pass out on the sidewalk not knowing if we had been there 2 minutes or 2 days. But the days of Quaaludes didn't last long; in a way I'm glad because I don't think I would still be alive to write this book if they had lasted any longer.

There was a time in high school when I was drawn to diet pills. There were all kinds of diet pills, referred to as speed or uppers. The first time that I took an upper I was talkative and felt very creative. It took away my hunger for food and gave me energy that I didn't know I had. After I had started taking diet pills, I felt as if I had taken my experimentation to a new limit. Now I was a speed freak. I had taken tranquilizers and now I was taking speed. "I was a pill popper."

The news had always reported how addictive diet pills were, how speed killed, how people would become dependent after taking them for an extended period of time. However I always thought that what happened to everyone else would not happen to me.

In the late seventies I started to experiment with acid, or L.S.D. (lysergic acid diethylamide), a strong drug that causes you to hallucinate after you ingest it. It had originally been made by a scientist to treat schizophrenia, but the effects that it would cause a normal person were out of this world.

It was fun and exciting but scary at the same time. I had heard so many stories about how you would feel after taking a dose of it. You would see pretty colors, and see beautiful things; but just as easily as you saw nice things you could see horrible things. You could have delusions of monsters or thoughts of dread ... but I wanted to try it anyway. Luckily for me I didn't have any bad trips or see any monsters or have the bad feelings.

But after I would take it, I would always have the thought of "maybe I shouldn't have taken it," because there was no turning back after placing a hit of it on your tongue or swallowing it. I would have that speedy feeling in the beginning, then I would start to hallucinate, then there was nothing I could do but ride the high out.

I would have visions of beautiful things. Pictures would seem come to life. I would see colors that were not there. I would see tracers when I would wave my hand in front of my face. I would spend hours watching things change shape and move around. And I would think that I had figured out the answers to life's most complicated questions.

I didn't realize how powerful L.S.D was. They didn't call it the drug that made you hear one hand clapping for nothing. Whenever I thought I couldn't get any higher I always did. I kept my sanity by telling myself that this couldn't last forever. I spent six years experimenting with L.S.D. Later on in life I would wonder if things would look the same to me if I had never taken it.

Through out the years I would experiment with all kinds of drugs from the time I was fourteen to the time I was thirty nine. I drank alcohol, smoked pot, took pills, dropped acid, tried MDA and THC, took psilocybin mushrooms, and any of the chemicals along the way. I enjoyed taking pills referred to as downers the most. I liked the relaxed feeling I would get after I took any kind of pill that was prescribed for pain, sleep, or anxiety. I loved how pills made me feel carefree and would make me feel comfortable around other people after I took them.

So much happens in your high school years; I used mine for experimentation, but I also did some of the normal things that teenagers do. I had gotten my driver's license when I was sixteen, I went to school dances, and I got my first job working at a gas station. Now I was eighteen and I was in my senior year and ready to graduate.

I had lived in Bardwell for almost all of the eighteen years of my life, and now I was old enough to be on my own. So in 1980 after I graduated, I loaded up my van and I moved from my home in Bardwell, Kentucky to Nashville, Tennessee.

# III
# Stage Six Of My Life

*My move to Nashville and my first job in Nashville*

Nashville is a much bigger city than where I was coming from. It is known as the Capital of Country Music. There are a lot of things to do in Nashville. Either there was a concert at the Grand Old Opry, or the Tennessee State Fair or something else going on. I spent many nights at the War Memorial building with my new pair of skates and my headphones. My headphones looked like giant earmuffs growing out of my head, because back then they only made the big bulky ones, the ones that had the radio and the antenna built into the ear piece and that took a nine volt battery. The battery compartment would constantly break, and in the end I would always find myself with a battery hanging from the two wires that connected it to the headphones.

Nashville has a skyline of tall buildings that seemed especially awesome to someone who grew up in a small town. It had the Life and Causality Building, which was Nashville's tallest building at that time. Now it is the ATT building. Then there's the Hyatt Regency Hotel which had a restaurant on top that rotated so that the patrons could enjoy the view of the city. There were many more buildings that made up Nashville's skyline, but those are the two that stand out in my mind. I loved seeing the city on a hill from a distance. It was fun seeing the big buildings from Highway 41; it meant that you were almost there. The anticipation of going to a big city and then seeing the buildings was quite unique.

When I first came to Nashville, I stayed with my older brother. Because of the excitement of being on my own and being in a different city, I wasn't abusing drugs and alcohol like I had done in Bardwell. I was using them, but not to the extent I had previously done. I was keeping my homosexual feelings deep inside; but it was only a matter of time before they would come to the surface and I would have to face them.

In the meantime, I got my first job cooking hamburgers and frying French fries at a Lendy's Restaurant. It was so exciting to get a job. I had worked at a gas station in Bardwell, but I guess living on my own and working just made things more exciting.

I worked with two girls at the restaurant who were looking for a roommate. The thought of moving into my own place seemed like a good move for me to make. Since I had been staying with my brother for six months already, I thought now would be a good time to start looking for my own place.

Sandra and Nancy, the girls with whom I worked, had a two bedroom apartment. They were looking for someone to sleep on the sofa so they could split the rent three ways. I decided to rent with them and sleep on the sofa.

Our first apartment was a trip; we had milk crates for shelves, and we would decorate with plants from the outside or anything we could get for free. We also had fish nets of all day glow colors that were for black lights hanging from the ceiling. They made the ceiling seem lower than it was. When you walked into a room you felt like you wanted to duck your head down because the fish nets hung so low. We had posters of various famous people hanging on the wall, and a bunch of these would glow when we turned on our black light. We also had a strobe light that would make everything seem in slow motion. Those lights were perfect for someone high on pot or tripping on acid, like I would be sometimes.

I would pay less than the two girls who had their own rooms. But after a year, Sandra (one of the girls with whom I worked and shared an apartment), moved out so it was only the other girl Nancy and I. I got my own bedroom, but Nancy and I would have to split the bills two ways so it was a lot more money. I could afford it at the time, so it worked out fine.

I continued working at Lendy's, but I hadn't told anyone about my gay feelings. I still didn't want anyone to know how I felt and subconsciously I didn't want to face it either.

After a couple of months of not abusing drugs and alcohol I started taking large amounts again. I was becoming depressed. The hiding of my true feelings and the thought of being on my own was causing me to go into a depression. You would think that the freedom of being on my own would make me elated, but with the pressure of everything that came along with it, it made me depressed. The drugs and alcohol made my mild depressions seem worse. I had been depressed in the past, but nothing like this.

# Stage Seven Of My Life

### *My first suicide attempt*

I got so depressed that I tried suicide for the first time. I cut both of my wrists and I tried to take an overdose of sleeping pills. I took a razor blade and I made a quick slicing motion across my arm. One of the places that I cut started to spurt blood, but I didn't pay attention as the warm blood from the other cuts ran down my arm. I was so high and drunk that I didn't care. I just kept on slicing! I was desperate, and I was trying to make sure that I cut enough to bleed to death. After I had made several cuts, I stopped. I thought it would be enough, but it wasn't.

Because of my actions I ended up being taken to a mental hospital. My first experience of a mental hospital was unforgettable. I felt like I was in a scene from a movie.

I was led up the sidewalk by my brother, I was groggy from the pills that I had taken, and my arms were throbbing from the pain where I had sliced them. My brother led me into the brick building in front of us. As we opened the doors the receptionist stared at me under her cat eye glasses as if I had done something wrong, or that I had (ring around the collar or something). The doctors saw me and acted as if it were nothing. Here I was with my arms cut up, and they acted as if it was something that happened all of the time. I guess they saw it everyday, so it was no big deal to them. I thought that they felt because of me they had to do more work. Even later on in my life whenever I have needed to get stitches from having sliced my wrists, I would never get the sympathy I expected from the doctors.

At the time, I was high on drugs and drunk on alcohol, so the doctors attributed my suicide attempt to the use of substances. The doctor stitched up my wounds and gave me anti depressants for my depression, and then he and his nurse released me into the custody of my brother. I went to various drug and alcohol programs, but I thought I was smarter than everyone there and didn't pay attention to what they were telling me. I stayed with my brother for a while until I was better. Then I told him I would never try that again, and that I was okay.

I went back to work at Lendy's; I had bounced back from my trying to kill myself. But I continue to abuse drugs, and alcohol.

To me my suicide attempt didn't seem like a big deal. I ignored what everyone was telling me, that it was the drinking and the drugs that were making my depression seem worse; I just hoped that I would never feel that low again. I went about my life as if nothing had ever happened.

# Stage Eight Of My Life

## *My first trip to Miami*

It was now 1981. My friend Sally who had come to Miami when she was sixteen had become a prostitute. Her family had come down here a couple of years later. She wanted me to come down. It was going to be her sister's birthday, and she wanted to surprise her sister with me being there. I hadn't seen her sister in years, and I thought it would be fun to come down to Miami. And since I had gotten my stitches out and was feeling better, I thought a trip would do me good.

I took a Grey Hound bus from Nashville and the trip on a bus seemed to take forever. I sat next to the window so I could enjoy the view. But for some reason, as soon as someone sat next to me and I knew I was blocked in, I would feel the urge to go to the bathroom. I could have stood up and used the bathroom anytime, but I felt the need to do so only when someone sat down and blocked me in. It's like as soon as your hands are covered by the smock they put on you, when you go to get a haircut and then you have to scratch your nose.

The fare on the bus was so cheap, and it was much more expensive to fly. Since I didn't have a lot of money it was a good economical way to travel.

I finally arrived at Maggie's in Miami; it happened so that I arrived on her birthday. She lived in a place called the Shacks; it was located off US-1, under State Road 826, about three blocks south of Kendall Drive. The Shacks "as it was referred to" was a building that consisted of four apartments. Maggie lived in the first unit, which was the biggest apartment; it had a kitchen, a living room, a bedroom and a bathroom.

There was a girl next to Maggie, next to her was another girl, and next to her were a couple of college boys. Their units only had one room and a bathroom. But when you are young that's all you need. At that place and time it was always one big party. I don't know if it was everyone's mind set or if it was the decade that we were living in, but it seemed everyone liked to party. I guess everyone was away from their parents and felt free.

I was still unsure of what I wanted to do with my life. I liked it down here, but I liked it up north too. I stayed in Miami about a month and then I went back to Nashville. I did not know what waited for me there, if anything.

# Stage Nine Of My Life

### *My trip back to Nashville*

After I arrived in Nashville, I started to get homesick about a place that wasn't even my home. I missed Miami and the friends that I had made there. I went back to work for Lendy's, but since I had traveled out of state I felt like I was more grown up than the people whom I worked or hung around with.

I was doing a lot of drugs and drinking a lot of alcohol at that time so I'm sure that contributed to the way I was acting. And I ended up getting fired from the job that I liked so much.

A couple of weeks later, I got a job down the street at a pizza place called Mr. Pizza. My friend Nancy was going back to school, so I thought that would be good for me too. I was a crazy acting nineteen year old, and I was willing to try anything. I went ahead and filled out the necessary applications to start school.

After a few months of working at Mr. Pizza, I started college at MTSU (Middle Tennessee State University). I knew I had to change the way I was acting. I quit my job, I cut down on my drug and alcohol use and I planned on concentrating on my studies.

The school I started to attend was located in Murphysboro, Tennessee. I didn't have a place to live so I slept in my van, which I parked in a campus parking lot. I would have to wake up earlier than everyone in the dorms so that I could use the showers there.

Thank God it wasn't cold yet; it was still autumn, so sleeping in my van wasn't that bad.

After a while of sleeping in my van, Nancy introduced me to this girl who was looking for a roommate and I moved in with her. We shared an apartment, but I didn't live there long.

From the pressure of trying to do well in school I started to use drugs and alcohol excessively again, and that was not a good idea. I applied and was approved for a student loan; however, most of the time I was broke from spending my money frivolously.

I ended up quitting school - I quit school for the silliest reason though. Whenever I went to class and it would be so quite that you could hear a pin drop, my stomach would growl; I would feel so embarrassed ... That was what I made a major life decision on. I packed up my van with the few belongings that I had and I drove from Murphysboro, Tennessee to Miami, Florida.

# Stage Ten Of My Life

### *My trip back to Miami*

After I left Murphysboro, I drove all night and then fell asleep in my van; but I guess I had gone around in circles because when I woke up I was in a parking lot in Atlanta, Georgia. Atlanta is only about 3 hours from Murphysboro. I got up and continued driving. I finally arrived to the warm weather of Miami. I didn't know what street to go on, so I called Sally's sister Maggie. She happened to live two blocks from where I was calling from, so she walked over, and met me. It was so good to see a friendly face. Maggie had married since the last time I was down for her birthday; her husband was a guy named Muhammad.

Muhammad was from Pakistan, he was a small sized man with dark skin, which he had inherited from his Pakistani ancestors. He was a responsible man who worked two jobs. Overall, he was a nice person; he made sure his bills were paid on time, and he was always a person of reason.

Muhammad and Maggie had a one bedroom townhouse off US-1 and Kendall Drive, two blocks away from the Shacks. It was in the apartments behind the old Mum's restaurant. (Mum's was a German style restaurant that was very popular in Miami). There are only a few, if any, left; most were closed years ago. I didn't know how long I was going to stay, "maybe for a couple weeks only." But, after I had been there a week, I knew that I wanted to stay in Miami longer. Muhammad and Maggie said that I could stay with them, but I had to help out with the groceries and the bills and stuff.

Maggie was only a year or two older than me; we had become friends in Bardwell. We got along perfectly with each other; I loved to party, and so did Maggie. Muhammad didn't party that much, but he would go out drinking with us on his days off.

Maggie and I stayed drunk most of the time. We could always find a reason to party. To us all occasions were special, and that provided a reason for us to get drunk. I was having a good time. If only at that time I had only known at what cost, things might have been different.

# Stage Eleven Of My Life

### *My first job in Miami*

In 1983 I started to work at Burger World on US-1 in Miami. It was only a few blocks from Muhammad's and Maggie's apartment. The job only paid minimum wage, but it was very easy. I did the morning shift, so I had to be there early to open the restaurant.

I started to think about my life again and what I wanted to do. I had quit school in Murphysboro, and here I was in Miami. I was using a lot of drugs and I was drinking a lot of alcohol. And I was still hiding my homosexual feelings.

Since I was more interested in drinking and doing drugs, and I was still very immature, my job at Burger World didn't last long. I just stopped going to work; I would rather sleep late, and then get up and go party.

# Stage Twelve Of My Life

## *My second job in Miami*

After I quit my job, I still had to buy food, pay for gas for my van, and help out with the bills. I got a job as a cook at the Mum's restaurant in Coconut Grove. Mum's had a family type work atmosphere; there were only a few employees, and everyone got along with each other. It was not a five star restaurant, but it was a step up from making breakfast at Burger World. I enjoyed working at Mums, and I enjoyed working in Coconut Grove too.

The Grove, as everyone called it, was a lot different than living in the part of Miami where I was staying. Even though it was only a few miles away, the atmosphere in the Grove was totally different.

The "Grovenites" who lived there were people who were very laid back; their main means of transportation were usually bicycles or roller skates. There were a lot of people from other places who would stop off in the Grove on their way to Key West to see how it was, and most of the people stopping off in the Grove ended up staying there or would come back there after they had visited Key West.

The Grove was a special place, especially if you liked to live like a hippie; the Grove was full of hippie-like people. It just had a different air about it. You could feel the difference in the air.

# Stage Thirteen Of My Life

## *My becoming friendly with Denise*

After I had been working in the Grove for a while, I became friendly with this girl named Denise, who was a waitress at Mum's. She was tall with curly hair and had a unique beauty about her.

I would give her a ride home after work, because she didn't have a car, only a bicycle. She lived in a small apartment on 27th avenue right off of Tigertail Avenue in the Grove. The apartment was very quaint; it was decorated with the type of stuff that you would see at a vintage store that sold stuff from the sixties. She listened to some cool albums and she even still had some eight track tapes even though they had gone out of style ten years before.

After I worked at Mum's for about a month, I started to go over to Denise's almost every night to party. On one of those nights she offered me this drug called zoom; it was a drug that you would inject. Even though I was scared, I tried it.

I bought a ten dollar capsule, and I bought a syringe. I dissolved the powder from the capsule in water, and then I injected it. I had gone from popping pills to injecting zoom I was going to go to hell in a hand basket.

Injecting the drug was not a pretty sight. I would have to find a vein in my arm that was good and easy to puncture. To do that I would have to wrap my upper arm with a belt or some thing that was long like a neck tie or something to make my veins in my lower arm pop out. I would then take the point of the needle and pierce my vein injecting the drug and wait for the sensation to go throughout my body. When I felt the rush that the zoom gave me, I would then know that I had injected the drug into my blood stream.

It would give you this fantastic rush for about 30 seconds; your ears would ring, the lights would whirl around your head, your mind would zoom. And then it would be over. Even though the high didn't last long, and even if you were tired, you would want to keep doing it over and over again. The process of injecting the drug, then coming down, and going to get another capsule could last all night.

Since I had been going over there almost every night and partying, Denise and I ended up going to bed with each other. I don't know how it happened, but it did. Even though I knew subconsciously that I was gay, I still went to bed with her.

# Stage Fourteen Of My Life

*Denise becomes pregnant and our wedding*

Denise got pregnant. After Denise found out she was pregnant we decide to get married. Our wedding was very unusual. We were married by Denise's brother's ex-wife, who was a notary public. We had our wedding at my friend Sally's house.

Maggie and Sally set up chairs in the Florida room for the people who came to the wedding to sit in. They decorated the best that they could. Overall, the Florida room, with all of its decorations looked like a place where someone was going to get married.

Denise's maid of honor was her friend; they had known each other since the age of sixteen. Denise and her friend used to go everywhere together. They had met at a restaurant where they were both waitresses and had a lot in common. But Denise hadn't seen her in a while. Her friend was trying to stay clean and sober; she had been arrested recently for a DUI, and she hadn't been around in a while. I guess our wedding was not the place to stay sober because she ended up getting drunk on the champagne before the wedding ceremony began.

The maid of honor dropped the wedding ring that she was supposed to hand Denise. She started to cry saying over and over - in her slurred drunk voice – and using explicative language that one would not use in everyday life, that she had ruined Denise's wedding. She was so drunk that Denise had to get the ring from the floor herself.

My best man was a good friend of my friend Sally. (I wasn't close to anyone down here; I was friends with Maggie's husband, but I think he was working). Anyway, I needed a best man, and Sally's friend said that he would stand up with me.

It was the early eighties, but when my best man came out of the back room he was dressed like he was a pimp from the seventies. He was a skinny Afro American man, and he was wearing a fedora hat with a long feather sticking out of the side. He also had on a bright yellow shirt, with bright yellow pants. He had been in the bedroom "getting ready." By getting ready I mean he had been in there snorting coke, so by the time he came out and made his appearance, the ceremony had already begun.

We had our wedding, even with the maid of honor dropping the ring, the best man appearing late, someone hitting their head on a lamp as they stood up to clap when the vows had finally been said, and someone else's yelling when their money came up missing. Through all of that chaos we were finally married.

# Stage Fifteen Of My Life

### *The honeymoon*

After the wedding we tried to find a motel room for the honeymoon. I was nervous while we were looking. I had stayed sober for our wedding, and now I didn't know how to get myself in the mood. I had bought a bottle of whisky to drink after the wedding, but that wasn't enough to block out the feelings I had of another man. I didn't want Denise to think that she wasn't attractive so I stalled as long as I could. I made up excuse after excuse.

There was a big fight going on in the room next door. Denise was so entertained from the commotion, and it was so late that we just went to sleep. She never questioned me about not making love that night. I had dodged a bullet, but deep down I think she knew of my true feelings.

After our honeymoon was over, we went back to our lives in the Grove for a month or two. Then we moved into a mobile home in University Lakes Trailer Park.

# Stage Sixteen Of My Life

### *Our first home*

It wasn't the nicest trailer park in Miami, but it wasn't the worst one either. I didn't think I would like living in a trailer, because the walls were so thin. The summer sun in Miami could be so hot. But with the use of air-conditioning it wasn't that bad.

Living in the mobile home park was like living in a small community. Everybody knew everybody else. Most of the people who lived there were like us, getting a mobile home first and planning on getting a house later on. It was a nice trailer on a corner lot; it was located at the end of a cul-de-sac. We made our first home as comfortable as possible. Denise was six months pregnant at the time, and the pregnancy was going good.

Since we didn't have a lot of money, and my job didn't provide health insurance, Denise had to give birth at Lackson Memorial Hospital. Lackson is a public hospital in Miami where people with low income jobs could go. The hospital was very crowded, it wasn't as nice as some of the hospitals in Miami, but it was all we could afford at the time.

# Stage Seventeen Of My Life

### *Our first child*

My son was born on October 14th 1984. It was a life changing experience. I witnessed a life being born; I got to cut the umbilical cord. I was just elated.

The first few months were fun, because parenthood was a new experience, but after a couple of months it was like I had been doing it my whole life. I was still abusing drugs and alcohol, but not a lot. I had cut down when Mark was born because he took up so much of my time. I didn't want to face the fact that I was living a lie so I kept myself preoccupied. I put all of my attention into raising our son Mark. It was a way of not having to face my feelings.

# Stage Eighteen Of My Life

### *My third job in Miami*

I was still working at Mum's in Coconut Grove. But since we had moved in to the mobile home which was on 127th Avenue (opposite side of town from the Grove), I had to drive a long way. I was trying to get a job closer to where we lived. I went on an interview, and I finally got a job as a cook at Benny's Restaurant on 97th Avenue and Flagler Street. Again I felt like it was a step up from the places that I had worked before.

I went through the training they offered and did really well. The managers liked me, and I got along well with everyone with whom I worked. The job offered good insurance, and it turned out it was an interesting place to work.

I met this lady who worked as a waitress. She and I became

friends. She knew I liked to take pills, so she introduced me to her son in law who sold pills on the side of his other business of selling cocaine. He then introduced me to a lady who owned a pharmacy and sold pills illegally.

I liked going to the pharmacy, because I liked going behind the counter, where I could see all the different bottles and colors of pills. I would get this good feeling from just seeing them.

There I could buy pills by the hundreds; I could get pain pills, sleeping pills, diet pills, tranquilizes and any other pill that I wanted for any ailment. I felt as if I had hit the jackpot! Being able to get any kind of pill I wanted was a drug addict's dream come true. I started to abuse drugs again. With the access I had and not having the willpower to say no, I went hog wild.

I met another person at the restaurant where I worked with whom I would become friends. Peter was the dishwasher. He was a nice guy, he was not gay and I wasn't attracted to him sexually. We got along well. He became addicted to pain pills when he went to serve in Vietnam ten years before.

He was very smart, I always thought that if he used his knowledge for something good he would have probably owned a company, or have been someone in a high position.

We both liked to take pills for their effect, and he had many different ways to get them. For the next several years we would trade pills and find ways to obtain them.

With Peter's smarts we came up with a scam where we could get all the pills we wanted for free. "I still hadn't progressed to the large amounts that I would take later in my life." But it was just a matter of time.

Peter gave me a pill called Fiorinal #3 for the first time. It was prescribed for pain, but it had a lot of other chemicals in it. It had a barbiturate that made you sleepy, a stimulant that gave you energy, and a pain reliever to take the anxiety away.

Peter was prescribed these pills for migraine headaches, and I would trade him a prescription of Anexia D pills, which I would sometimes get for pain, for a prescription of Fiorinal #3 pills. I liked Fiorinal #3 a lot better at that time, but later on I would become addicted to hydrocodone bitrate, the chemical that is in Anexia-D.

I would later start taking a pill called Vicodin ES because it had the same chemical and was widely prescribed at that time.

At first Anexia-D pain pills didn't affect me; they where in no way as good as Fiorinal #3. But after taking the Anexia-D pills for a while, (because I didn't have Fiorinal #3), I began to like the feeling I got from them even more.

I liked the feeling that I got after I took any kind of narcotic for pain. I liked the way they would take away the stress I felt in my back. And I liked the way they would make me feel, like I didn't have a care in the world.

Knowing that I had a full bottle of pills made me feel good. I know the feeling was in my mind, but the feeling would be a good feeling until the bottle of pills would be almost empty.

I hated the withdrawal feelings I would get when I ran out of pills; I would lay there with my heart pounding, and sometimes it felt as though my heart was going to beat right out of my chest. I would have diarrhea, then I would have body cramps, and I would get tired and want to sleep.

I would have flu like symptoms for three days, and then my withdrawals would be over. Withdrawing from pain pills was becoming my normal routine. I would spend all week taking pills to get high, and all weekend getting off of them. I don't know when I became addicted. One day I was buying pills for experimental purposes, but before I knew it I was addicted to them. Mark was getting older, so he didn't need all of the attention that I was focusing on him. Denise became pregnant again, during one of my binges we conceived another baby.

# Stage Nineteen Of My Life

*My second suicide attempt*

Because of everything I was beginning to get depressed again. I guess the gay feelings that I was having, and trying to live a life of being married to a person of the opposite sex was finally getting to be too much pressure for me to handle. It was at this time I attempted suicide again.

Since slicing my wrist and taking an overdose of pills hadn't worked, I thought I would try carbon monoxide poisoning, I had always heard that the gas emitted from the tail pipe of a car would cause you to die quietly.

I drove the car to a store parking lot, I attached a vacuum cleaner hose to the tail pipe of my car, and then I started the car and waited. Normally you would just fall asleep, but the car got full of exhaust fumes, and the only things that I got were two watery eyes and a bad cough.

I know it looked comical with me attaching a hose to my tail pipe, in the middle of a [Dinn Wixie] parking lot, but it really was not. I wanted to die at that point in my life, the knowledge that slicing my wrist, taking an overdose, or carbon monoxide poisoning didn't work caused me to go into a deeper depression. The worst feeling to have is the feeling of having no way out.

I went on with my life of taking drugs and drinking, hoping that it would get better by itself, but subconsciously I knew that it wouldn't.

# Stage Twenty Of My Life

### *Our second child*

Denise was going to give birth any day now. I was working for Benny's and I had good insurance. So when she went into labor and gave birth to Samantha Kay, on December, 26 1985, she gave birth at Maptist Hospital, a private hospital in Miami.

Now I not only had a son to occupy myself with but I had a daughter to keep me busy as well. Everything seemed good from the outside looking in, but trying to pretend that everything was okay just made things worse.

In my mind I just pretended that the suicide attempt never happened. I was getting good at convincing myself of what I wanted to believe. I pretended that my depression would just go away on its own. I know that wasn't realistic, but to someone taking as many drugs as I was, it seemed as if were possible.

# Stage Twenty One Of My Life

### *Taking my drug use up a notch*

Taking pills or alcohol wasn't affecting me like it did in the beginning; my tolerance level had been built up. I wanted something stronger so I started abusing stronger drugs; I even started injecting heroin. I didn't mind injecting drugs because I had done it in the past.

My drug use was becoming more intense. I had become addicted to pills. Between the pills I obtained through my scam and those I got from the pharmacy, I was able to take as many as I wanted; but my addiction to other drugs would soon come.

# Stage Twenty Two Of My Life

### *Our second home*

One thing that kept me going was the fact that we were looking for a house to move into. Even with my drug and alcohol use and everything that I was going through, I would still pretend everything was ok.

We had lived in the trailer for almost two years and after looking at numerous houses we had finally found one. It was the Christmas season, so it would be a perfect way to end the year.

I had quit my job at Benny's on Christmas Day, six days before the scheduled closing for the house. It wasn't the smartest thing that I had done, and it only made me have more stress. I was afraid that my not having a job would affect the closing, so Denise and I kept my quitting a secret.

I took a lot of pills before we went to the closing, so by the time the meeting was taking place, I was higher than a kite. I didn't want to risk saying something stupid so I didn't speak. Somehow we managed to close on our new house on December 31, 1986 – New Year's Eve.

Getting the house made me feel so good. I don't know if it was because of the drugs I was on, or because if it was because it was something new; but I liked the feeling I got when the house became ours. Right after the closing we went to the new house and looked around. Later on that night, we moved our belongings to our new house. The house was in the Perrine area, and would be a perfect place to raise a family. There were a few families who had children and lived a couple of houses down, so I knew it would be a good area for the kids to grow up.

All I would have to do for the perfect life is keep my gay feelings suppressed, hope that my depressions would not get worse, get a job and start working.

# Stage Twenty Three Of My Life

### *My fourth job in Miami*

About a month after we moved into the house I got a job at Kennigan's Restaurant working in the kitchen as a cook. Again I felt it was another step up. Even though I was still a line cook, it was a nicer kitchen, and I could move up the ladder.

After I worked there a while, I was promoted and I started to train cooks who were training to become managers. They had to learn the different aspects of the restaurant. They had to learn everything from being a waiter/waitress, to learning how to bus tables. I was the one who taught them about the kitchen.

I was taking various pills, but most of the time I was taking Fiorinal #3 pills; even though I liked the Anexia D pills better, I liked the energy the Fiorinal gave me. My withdrawal symptoms became more frequent. I had suffered withdrawals from pain pills before, but since I had always thought that tranquilizers were not addictive I never ever tried to stop taking them.

I tried not to run out of pills, I had built my tolerance level up to where I was taking anywhere from fifty to seventy pain pills a day. I know it seems impossible to take that many pills, but to an addict with a tolerance level like mine it is not. I was also taking tranquilizers to even out the speedy feeling I would get from Fiorinal. Between all of the pills that I was taking, most people would have overdosed and died.

# Stage Twenty Four Of My Life

### My first trip to rehab

I checked myself into Blenn Bay, a rehabilitation hospital. (A rehabilitation hospital is a hospital that you could go to withdraw from drugs or to work on any serious problem that caused you to act destructively). Almost everyone knows what a rehab hospital is from all of the press and from such shows as "Intervention" or "Celebrity Rehab." This would be the second hospital that I had been in so far in my life.

Before I was admitted I was interviewed by a staff member to see how serious my problem was. I was scared that my problem wasn't bad enough to be admitted, but once they saw the condition that I was in they admitted me right away.

First I was taken to the closet medical hospital in case I needed medical attention. The discontinuance of taking pills was life threatening for me. The staff wanted me to have the medical attention that I might need.

The doctors at the medical hospital had brought my level down to where I was not taking any pain pills, but they were still giving me small amounts of tranquilizers hoping to wean me from them slowly.

I stayed at the medical hospital for about a week and then I was transferred back to the rehabilitation hospital to begin my recovery. I never really got off the tranquilizers; even though they were weaning me off of them slowly, I had some hidden in my drawer. And since they expected to find tranquilizers in my system, they only checked for pain pills and barbiturates in the urine test. I had already detoxed from the pain pills so that was no problem.

Denise and the kids would come to visit once a week, but we would only get to spend an hour together. I didn't talk about my depression or my gay feelings, and the hospitals philosophy was to be open and to be truthful. I wasn't being honest with myself or anyone else, so it really wasn't doing me any good.

I did the program at the rehabilitation hospital, but my sobriety did not last long, only about two weeks. I got out feeling like a new person; I was clean and sober from the pain pills for the first time, but I was still taking tranquilizers again without the doctors' knowledge. But after a couple of weeks I started doing the same drugs that I had been doing when I admitted myself. If you don't fix the problem that caused you to use in the first place, you will go back to the same habits you had to begin with.

# Stage Twenty Five Of My Life

*My first gay experience*

After I had been out of the hospital a couple of months, I had my first gay experience. I had never experimented with my homosexuality before, but that was about to change.

Denise and I would go to this park to roller skate and one day when we went to the park, this man came jogging by. He was very good looking, and he winked at me. I took Denise and the kids home, and I went back hoping that the man would still be there. And he was. I was so nervous ... I was inexperienced; it was the first time ever I was with a man, and I felt like a school boy with a crush. I felt I was finally acting on the feelings that I had been suppressing for so long. I continued to meet with him for about a month. I realized then that I wanted to spend the rest of my life in a homosexual relationship, but it turned out that this man wasn't looking for that.

# Stage Twenty Six Of My Life

*My third suicide attempt*

From the pressure of being with another man, while at the same time trying to keep it a secret, and from all of the drug use, I became deeply depressed again, and I attempted suicide for the third time.

This time I sliced my wrist vertically and horizontally, I had heard that if you wanted to make sure you would die then you should cut your wrist vertically. I gushed blood the same from the vertical wounds as I did from the horizontal ones. This was becoming ridiculous; either I wasn't doing something right or it just wasn't my time to die.

Denise called an ambulance and I was admitted to the hospital. Like they had done in the past, the doctors numbed my wounds, so that when they gave me stitches I wouldn't feel anything. They stitched up the wounds, prescribed me antidepressants, and sent me home. They gave me the names of different places to go get help with depression, but I thought it would be a waste of time. As far as I was concerned I didn't need help from anyone.

Once I'd sober up after a suicide attempt I would feel stupid and I would just pretend to myself that the suicide attempt had never happened. For some reason I got the courage to carry out the suicide attempts when I was under the influence. I probably wouldn't have tried the first time back in Tennessee if I hadn't been wasted.

Denise was working as a waitress at another restaurant. Since I didn't have a job, because after the brief stint at rehab, I quit my job, the pressure was getting to me so I started taking any type of drug that I could get.

The pharmacy where I had been buying my pills had been sold, but the new owner continued to let me buy pills there. And I also continued to get pills through my scam. There was a lady who worked the front counter who would steal pills from the pharmacy and she would sell them to me at a cheaper price. She would get me anything I wanted; I just had to call her and tell her what I needed. Then she would meet me outside to do the transaction.

Later, instead of me having to go to the pharmacy, she would take bottles of pills home, and I would eventually buy them directly from her. Since I wasn't working and I could only get so many pills from the scam (which was like a full time job it self), Denise had to pay for any extra pills we bought.

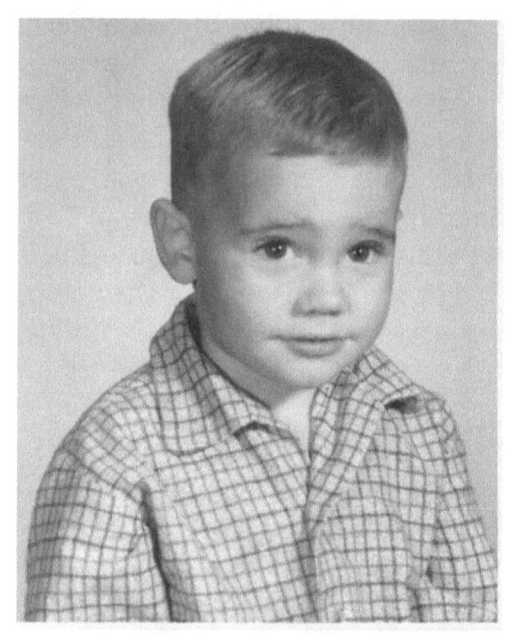

*Me at 4 or 5 years old*

*Me with Santa age approximately 6*

*6th Grade School picture*

*My Early Teens*

*Me on speed in a cemetary in Clinton*

*Me stoned in my late teens*

*Me stoned in the snow in my late teens*

*My graduating picture*

*Me tripping on acid in my car*

*Me playing around on my roommates motorcycle
in Nashville, Tennessee*

*Me playing around in the dumpster
in Nashville, Tennessee*

*Me tripping on strawberry mescaline
in Nashville, Tennessee*

*My first trip to Miami Fl., drinking a beer at the shacks*

*Me locked out on the roof of the Coral Gables court house*

*Me and the van I came to Miami Fl. in*

*Me outside of our first home in the mobile home lot.*

*Me outside our first home, getting mail.*

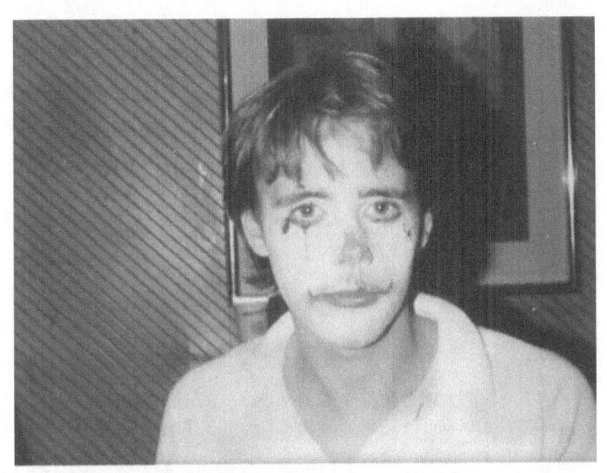

*Me with makeup still on after a Halloween party at work*

*Me after a day at the beach*

*Me goofing around one Halloween*

*Me with a glass of coke and whiskey*

*My first trip to rehab*

*Me dressed as a ghost one Halloween*

*Me by the Christmas tree in our second home.*

*Me at the condo in Kendall*

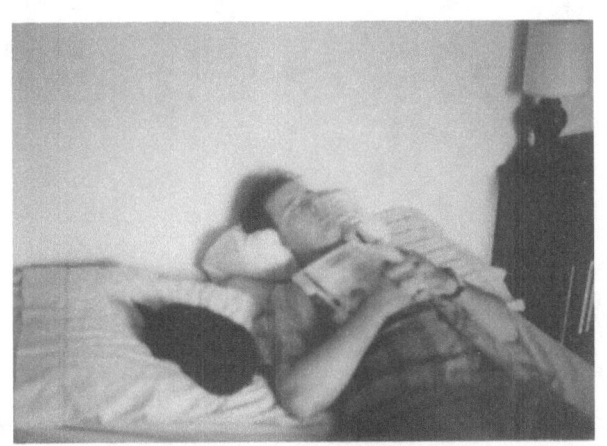

*Me asleep in Kendall*

*A trip to Kentucky to visit my mom*

*Me in my van on my way to work*

*Me in the trows of addiction to pills.*

*Me with a Santa suit on in Kendall*

*Me sitting by the pool in Kendall*

*Me having drinks*

*Me getting ready for a night on the town.*

*Me at work on my birthday*

*Me at one of the awards party my company threw*

*Me at another awards party*

*Me at another awards party, I had cut my hair,*
*I guess I was a supervisor now.*

*Me looking healthy*

*Me at a buffet on a cruise*

*Me wasted on pills on a cruise*

*Me in Mexico*

*Me after I started to party in Mexico*

*Me at dinner on a cruise*

*Me resting in my room on a cruise*

*Me in Key West*

*Me in New York*

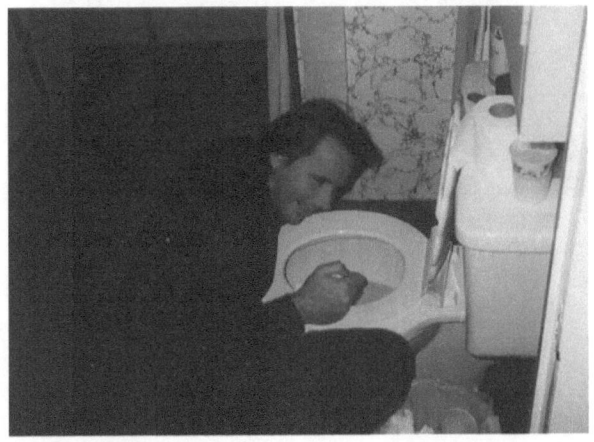

*Me making myself throw up so that I could drink more alcohol*

*Me at Ricardos moms house, after I had stopped*
*drinking and taking drugs*

*Me at the Metro rail station in Miami*

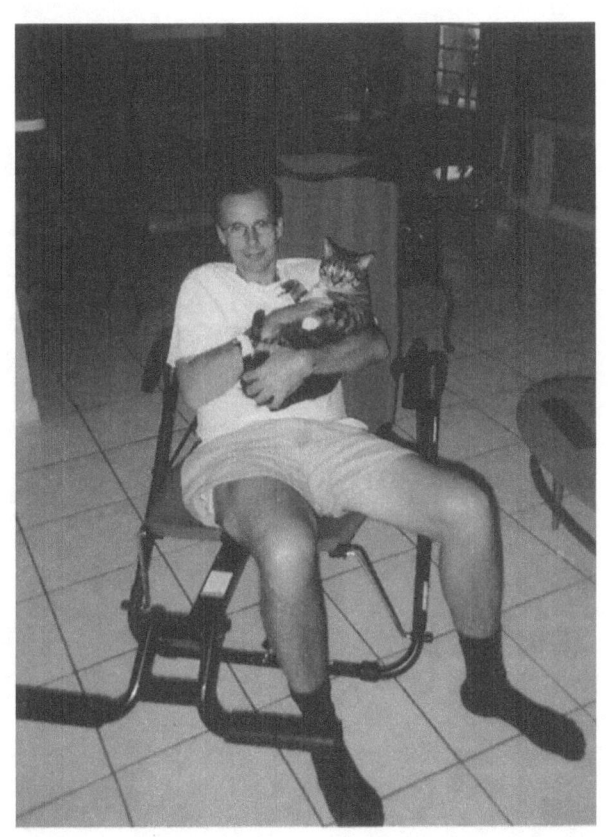

*Me in my ablounger, with my cat Juanita*

*Me on Lincon road for my 41st birthday*

*Me in Everglades City*

*Me by a bush cut into the shape of an 88, I thought it was neat.*

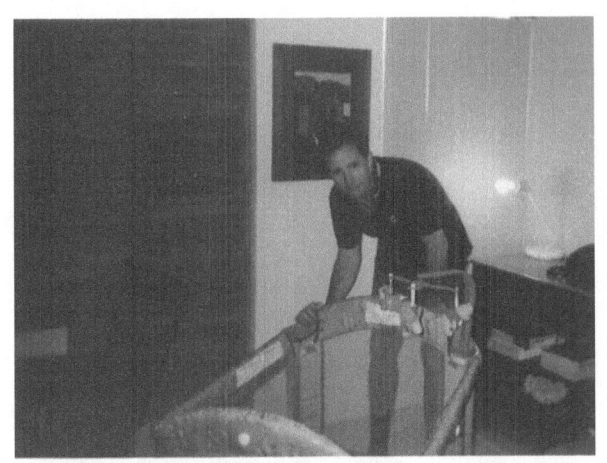

*Me by my first granddaughters play pen*

*My first day of Spanish*

*Some friends that I met in Spanish One*

# Stage Twenty Seven Of My Life

*My first experimentation with crack*

I started to experiment with crack. I was so used to how the pills were going to make feel, that I now wanted something different.

Crack cocaine was a form of cocaine that could be smoked. It is usually bought ready for use on the streets, but someone told me that all I had to do was to heat powder cocaine, mixed with water and baking soda, and get a small rock called base. I would then smoke this rock that I got from cooking the cocaine.

I think the process of transforming powder cocaine into base was just as addictive as smoking it. The feeling that I would get from smoking crack was indescribable, and the paranoia that came with it was terrible. I spent many nights looking out the window through a little peephole that I had made in the curtains. And God forbid if I dropped a rock of cocaine on the floor, I would spend the night looking for it. You would think I had OCD (obsessive compulsive disorder) or some other behavioral condition. I felt like when I was back in school and the teacher erased everything but one spot on the blackboard; I would want to jump up and erase the spot she had left but I never did.

I didn't like the feeling it gave me so I don't know why I did it in the first place. For some reason I would crave it and once I had started smoking it, I wanted to keep doing it all night.

One day while I was under the influence of crack I told Denise about my gay feelings. I didn't want to live having the feelings I was having without her knowing. I thought that since I had told someone about my gay feelings, I wouldn't get depressed anymore, but I was wrong.

# Stage Twenty Eight Of My Life

### *My fourth suicide attempt*

I did become depressed and I took an overdose of pills expecting to die! I started taking pills, ten at a time, until they were all gone. I took all the one hundred pain pills that were in the bottle. All the pills didn't dissolve in my stomach and I had built up such a high tolerance that they had very little effect on me. I called Denise at work and told her of what I had done; she came home and called an ambulance to take me to the hospital.

The doctors needed to pump out the contents of my stomach to get the extra drugs out. They put a tube about a quarter inch thick down my throat. It was so uncomfortable. This was the first time I was going to have my stomach pumped. It is something that I wish I never had to experience.

I didn't have health insurance at the time, so I was released after they had pumped my stomach. As with all of my suicide attempts, nothing ever came of it. I just pretended that it never happened and went on with my life.

I was still confused about the gay tryst that I had in the park. I was also conflicted about telling Denise about my true feelings. I was still unemployed. Denise was working as a waitress, and I knew that I needed to start working soon. But I didn't know what I wanted to do.

# Stage Twenty Nine Of My Life

### *Going to a gay bar*

I was looking for work, but in the meantime I started going to a gay bar on Bird Road called Carly's. I had finally decided to seek out the gay lifestyle. I had cut down on the drugs that I was taking, but I started to drink more alcohol.

The bar that I would go to was on 37th avenue and Bird road. It was a bar where gay men and gay women would meet for Happy Hour. I don't know what made me decide to go there, but I did.

Going to a gay club was a new experience for me. I was scared at first. I thought the bar would be dark and dirty, but it wasn't anything like I pictured it to be. It was a normal looking place. It had the bar where you could sit and have a drink. There were pinball machines in the back, and there was also a dance floor, that would be utilized late at night, when disco songs would blast frm the speakers.

The regulars would come in for Happy Hour just like at any other bar. Denise didn't want me to take the car, because one crazy night I had lost all four tires somewhere along the way and driven it home on just the rims. So she would drive me to the bar and drop me off; since I was not working yet, she would also give me money to spend. Life was really weird at that time.

# Stage Thirty Of My Life

### *My fifth suicide attempt*

I was still living at the house with Denise. And since Denise knew about my gay feelings, it made day to day life much easier. But since I was drinking a lot, it affected the way I thought about things, and I attempted suicide again.

I went into a deep depression and I slit my wrist. Denise called an ambulance, and they took me to the hospital again. After they stitched up my wounds, they made me stay in the hospital. This time it was mandatory that I stay for three days; under some law I was automatically kept there.

The three days seemed to last forever. I did arts and crafts, and watched TV to keep myself busy. I went to the group meetings and attended anything that was on the calendar. It could have been a lot worse. Here I was, without insurance and in a nice hospital getting good care. If someone had checked about my insurance, I would have ended up in a hospital of inferior quality and gotten horrible care; and that would have sucked.

# Stage Thirty One Of My Life

### *My first gay relationship*

After I got back home and recovered from my suicide attempt, I went back to the gay bar that I had previously been frequenting. I met this guy named Bradley. Bradley was an all around nice guy. He was the first guy I ever had a relationship with; other than the guy at the park, I had never experimented with my gay feelings. I was really confused at that time, I had stopped drinking, but I was taking a lot of drugs again, the exact opposite of when I started going to the bar. Here I was, still unemployed, having sex with a man, and married to a woman. I had built up my tolerance level again and I was taking at least thirty pain pills a day on top of the tranquilizers that I was taking. I was doing heroin off and on (I had previously dabbled with heroin when I lived in the trailer park), and I would take anything else that came my way.

Bradley had to go back up north to work. I continued going to the bar not knowing how I was going to spend the rest of my life. Then, in late 1990 I met the person with whom I am still today, 19 years later: Ricardo.

# Stage Thirty Two Of My Life

*Meeting the love of my life*

Ricardo was born in Cuba, but grew up in Puerto Rico. He was coming into the bar to have a few drinks and to socialize with his co-workers. He had a good personality, and we hit it off right away.

He was sitting next to me and we started to talk, we found that we had so much in common. He made me laugh and he was also very smart. I had always hung out with people who either made me laugh, or people who I could learn something from; now I had found someone that could do both. I moved into Ricardo's apartment within two weeks. I introduced him to Denise, they hit it off right away, and Denise told me if I was going to be gay, that she was glad that I had met Ricardo.

After moving in I realized living in a condo was much more different than living in a house. I felt the pressure of having to take care of the house, lift from my shoulders. It was the first time in a long time that I was not depressed.

Since I didn't have all of the stress that I had before, I decided to try to stop taking drugs. For the first couple of days that I lived with Ricardo, I was going through withdrawals. However my life without taking narcotics didn't last long. I guess I was scared about starting a new life, and I didn't handle it well, because I started using drugs, only a week after having decided to stop taking them.

# Stage Thirty Three Of My Life

### *Matt*

Before I had moved out, Denise and I were renting one of the bedrooms at the house we had in Perrine to a guy who worked at the same restaurant as Denise. His name was Matt, and he got along well with the kids. I guess when Matt found out what Denise was going through, with me going to a gay bar, moving in with a man, and wanting a gay relationship, he decided to console her because within a week of my leaving they were sleeping in the same room.

Matt was a serious person, the kind of person who would make sure everything was taken care of, and that the bills were paid on time. He was in his early twenties; even though he acted older he still hadn't experienced a lot of life yet.

He was a good man who was good to the kids and was good to Denise. He was taking on a lot; he was taking on the responsibilities of helping to raise the kids. And he also took on the financial burden of paying the bills at the house, something that I had never been good at. I was always finding myself in a bind, and Denise and I would have to ask Denise's mother for financial help.

# Stage Thirty Four Of My Life

### *My fifth job in Miami*

I didn't have any skills, other than the skills that it took to work in a restaurant. I wanted to work in one of the offices downtown. I wanted to wear a suit and tie. I wanted to be like the executives I would see. I wanted to feel important. I didn't care what position

I had as long as I worked in an office environment. I was tired of working as a cook in a kitchen. I would do anything as long as it didn't involve a hot stove or a deep fryer.

I got an office job with a temporary agency, I was so happy! Even though the job consisted of doing clerical duties and light office work, I felt I was important. Working for the temporary agency I would stay at a place as long as they needed me for that job. Then I would go to the next job or wherever they would need workers to go.

Working for the temporary agency was perfect, I was able to do that job, and be able to take my drugs and not be noticed. If I was, it wouldn't matter, because I would be sent to another job site as soon as that job was over, to work with a whole different group of people. I met my best friend (Martha, to whom I dedicate this book) at a job through the temporary agency. I also made some of my other closest friends there.

By this time in my life, I made sure I had a good supply of different pills. I didn't want to start withdrawing by accident. I would have red pills, white pills, blue pills, long pills, round pills, etc. How I felt would depend on which pill I would take, because some were uppers, some were downers, while others were for pain. I enjoyed taking the downers more, but sometimes I would need to take an upper when I became too sleepy from the other pills.

I worked for the temporary agency for about a year. Then I got my first full time job at an answering service. I worked at the answering service a few months, and then we were hit by Hurricane Andrew in August 1992.

# Stage Thirty Five Of My Life

### *Hurricane Andrew*

Going through a hurricane is like going on an LSD trip. It starts off slow but gradually intensifies. The winds start to blow and it will start to sprinkle rain. Then the winds would start blowing hard and the sprinkles of rain would turn into downpours.

The rain that would usually go straight down is now being blown by the wind and is going sideways. Every time you think it can't get any stronger it does. This may last for hours.

Basically, the same thing happens on an LSD trip; the high starts off slow and then intensifies. As soon as you think you can't get any higher you do.

In a hurricane, there's a time when the wind stops blowing hard, the rains stop pouring down; the sun may even come out. It's as if the storm is over. But it's because the eye of the storm is directly above you.

The eye is the center of the storm and is the calmest part of the storm, but it can be the deadliest because it can fool you into thinking that the storm is over.

Suddenly the winds begin to blow again and the rain starts to pour once more, but the winds are coming from a different direction than they were before; now you have to ride out the other side of the hurricane.

When we were hit by Hurricane Andrew it was one of the worst hurricanes to hit the United States. I was living with Ricardo in Kendall. There was little if any damage done to the condominium. The building we were in was shielded by the other buildings surrounding it, so it was not hurt.

The hurricane really did a number on the house though. The house was in the Perrine/Cutler Bay area and the area was hit hard. The porch was gone, the furniture was destroyed, and most of the trees outside had fallen. It looked like a bomb had been dropped in the front yard and destroyed everything that was within a 20 foot radius.

From what I could tell it looked like the wind had blown out a window, taken a piece of furniture, and thrown it around the room destroying everything in its way. I lost a lot of pictures and memories in that hurricane, things I could never get back. But Denise lost a lot more, she lost her mind.

# Stage Thirty Six Of My Life

*Denise's first symptoms*

I didn't realize that the hurricane affected Denise so much, but I guess it did. I was going down to Perrine to help out with the kids and we needed to fix the house from the damage from the hurricane.

I asked Denise about the check from the insurance company and she said that it had not come yet. Later on I found it hidden at the bottom of her purse. That was the first sign that something was wrong with her mind. I just ignored Denise's symptoms hoping that they would just go away, but again in the back of my mind I knew they wouldn't.

# Stage Thirty Seven Of My Life

*My sixth job in Miami*

In the meantime I started working for Star Cruises, and I liked my new job very much. Even after I took large amounts of drugs or drank large amounts of alcohol, I was still one of the best employees my boss had ever seen. I worked in the reservations department answering phones. There I would have to try to sell cruises and make the reservation over the phone. It was fun and easy to do.

About six months after working there I was promoted to the credit card approval desk, where I would call the different credit card companies and get an approval code for the credit cards that were used to pay for the trips.

A couple of months after that I was promoted to a supervisory position. Even though it meant I would make more money, it also meant that I would have more responsibility; which always meant that to handle it I would consume more drugs and alcohol.

I met this lady at work who knew someone who owned a pharmacy. With my scam I could only get pills classified under Schedule III or higher; but with the connection of the pharmacy I could get Schedule II pills. (Substances are rated by the Drug Enforcement Agency and assigned to schedules ranging from I to V. The more controlled a substance is, the lower the schedule number under which it is classified). The other pharmacy that I got pills from had long since been out of business.

With the ability again to have access to any kind of pill I wanted, and being able to get all the pills I could afford, I started taking larger amounts. Since I was making more money I could afford more expensive drugs as well.

Since I was taking so many pills I had to find ways to obtain them, other than my scam and the lady at work. I found a way. Older people would sell me the pills they didn't want; that way, they would have a little extra income and I would have my supply of the pills that I needed. I found all kinds of people to sell me their extras. I even bought pills from an ice-cream truck, one of those trucks that would drive through your neighborhood playing music to lure the awaiting children. Well, while the kids were buying their ice-cream, I would be in the back of the truck counting pills. (What I was capable of doing for my addiction)

I started to take way too many drugs, and my boss suggested that I try rehab once more. I went into a rehab hospital again and I was weaned off the pills slowly, but by the time I was clean and sober it was time for me to go home.  I went home and the first thing that I did was take a handful of pills. That defeated the purpose of my hospital stay. Needless to say that was a short lived sobriety.I went back to work for Star Cruises and continued working there as a supervisor.

# Stage Thirty Eight Of My Life

## *Denise is hospitalized*

During the time that I started working at the cruise line Denise was hospitalized for the first time. We put the hiding of the check, as well as all the other strange things she was doing into the back of our minds, hoping that it was our imagination. But it wasn't. She had stopped eating and she went down to ninety pounds.

We had her hospitalized and she seemed to be getting better, but deep down I knew that something was terribly wrong. I still hoped that it was nothing, but I would find out later how wrong I was.

After Denise was hospitalized, the doctors thought she might be suffering from some form of schizophrenia. Denise's walking had been affected from the medicine the doctors were giving her to treat her symptoms, and she started to limp on one side. It didn't seem like a big deal at the time, and she seemed better after taking the medication. So she was released, and went back home.

Matt was still at the house, and everything seemed okay. I helped out where I could, and the kids seemed fine or as fine as can be expected. Denise was back home; I was only hoping that it was a phase that she was going through. At that time I didn't know what was causing all of her problems. So I went back to live with Ricardo in Kendall.

After Denise was released from the hospital her mother was taking her to different doctors, until she was finally diagnosed with Vermian Syndrome. We knew what her symptoms where, but we did not know what caused them.

Apparently they were caused by the cerebellum of her brain having been eaten away by the drug Zoom that we had experimented with years before. Maybe she had gotten a bad batch of the drug; nobody knows.

Whenever Denise would be hospitalized I would go down to the house to help Matt take care of the kids. I guess I couldn't handle the stress of being responsible because I would start to take more drugs and drink more alcohol when I did. I was beginning to realize how bad our situation was. Denise was mentally sick, and I was a gay drug addict. I had two young children that were growing up, Matt helped as much as he could, but I could tell that with all the problems everything was taking a toll on him.

The doctors inserted a peg, which is a feeding tube, into Denise's stomach. With that she could get nutrition and I could give her the medicine she needed. She would eat and take her medicine by herself for a while. But then the sickness would take over and she would refuse to open her mouth. Then I would have to give her nutrients and medication through the tube.

Because of all of the stress that I was going through I started injecting heroin and cocaine on a daily basis. (I had started to use heroin and cocaine again when I got promoted and started making more money). I was also taking pills to get me through the day.

My drug addiction was out of control. I was taking thirty pain pills; and on top of that, I was taking ten tranquilizer pills a day for anxiety; so all together I was taking forty pills. That didn't include the other drugs I was doing.

During that time I was still working for Star Cruises. The cruise company grew from having thirty employees working on the phones to having sixty. I felt a lot of pressure due to the increased personnel that I would have to supervise. I wasn't under pressure from being gay, but now I was under pressure from my job.

I cut down on the amount of pills that I was taking, thinking that I was doing something good, but I was beginning to do more heroin. So the heroin increase was contradicting what I was trying to do. After a while I would only be doing heroin, and I would continue doing that for the next two years.

# Stage Thirty Nine Of My Life

### *Becoming addicted to heroin*

I became addicted to heroin, but I wasn't like the kind of heroin addict that I had always imagined: homeless, dirty, and crazy acting. I was employed and had a home and seemed rather normal. I didn't call in sick, but rather enjoyed going to work because I had told myself that I couldn't get high until I got to work, or that I could get high right before getting there.

If I had gotten high at home I knew I would have ended up being the stereotypical addict and I would never make it to work. Before I went to work I would drive to Coconut Grove and buy my heroin and my syringe there. I couldn't wait for the moment when I would get my fix. The daydreams of how the dope was going to make me feel made it where I didn't care what could happen, I could be arrested, or the dope might not be dope and doing it could kill me. Just knowing that I would be high soon made it worth all of the risks.

I fell into a routine of going to get my dope, using it, and then waiting for the next day so that I could do it over again. I had been doing that for two years. Then I decided to stop doing the heroin.

I went through the withdrawals, which were similar to pain pill withdrawals. I had withdrawn from pain pills numerous times before, and it wasn't much different. I had the usual back aches, diarrhea, and I would also crave the drug. That lasted a few days and then I was free from having to take the risk of going to get it. When I was using heroin the risk didn't bother me, but now the thought of being arrested makes me cringe. I stopped doing the heroin but I started taking a lot of pills.

The cruise company I worked for was sold to another cruise line. I went to the new company, but I only worked there a couple of months before I quit.

# Stage Forty Of My Life

## *Losing my mind to drugs and alcohol*

I worked at various office jobs, going to any place that was hiring. I was so addicted to drugs and alcohol at that point, that I couldn't hold a job. I would work for a company for a couple of months and then I would quit or get fired.

I started to drink heavily again. I stopped taking most of the drugs that I had taken in the past. Now I found that alcohol could make feel just as good as the drugs that I liked so much. I met my drinking buddy one night at a bar. She was well off money wise and had endless cash. We got along well because she liked to drink and to party like me.

# Stage Forty One Of My Life

## *Seizures*

Whenever I didn't have alcohol, I would have this strange feeling and I would start to see colors. That would be the onset of a seizure.

Every time I would stop drinking I would have a seizure. (A seizure is when your brain waves get mixed up and it causes an extra burst of energy that makes your body go into convulsions). I would also have seizures when I ran out of tranquilizers. So my seizures were very complex.

The doctors I saw about the seizures put me on this anti seizure medication called Dilantin. But taking the medication was worse than having a seizure because it had a lot of side effects. The medicine made me feel out of sorts; the lights would look brighter, I would have vivid dreams if I could sleep, or sometimes the medication would keep me awake at night.

Since I wasn't aware when I was having a seizure, I stopped taking the medication because I would rather have a seizure than suffer the side effects of the medication. I wasn't thinking right because if that happened to me today, I would put up with any kind of side effect to keep from having a seizure.

# Stage Forty Two Of My Life

### *Drugs and Alcohol taking over my life*

My behavior was erratic. I was living at the condo in Kendall, but when I drank I would want to stay where the alcohol was. I knew I could get alcohol at Maria's, (Maria is the girl with a lot of money whom I had met at the bar). So I would stay at her house whenever I was on a drinking binge. I would stay out drinking for days and then I would start to sober up and then I would go back home again, I kept up that routine for about a year.

During this time I would get so drunk that I would fall down steps. I've broken three ribs in my back. I would wake up after passing out on a bench surrounded by police officers; I would pass out in front of my front door after spending countless amounts of energy trying to get home. There was a time that I frequented a bar across from where I lived and when I was walking home one night I got hit by a car, but I was so drunk I didn't know anything had happened. I also found myself in jail quite often during these times.

I had been to jail in the past, but nothing to this extent. I would get out of jail in the morning and be in jail again that same day at night. That is how crazy the binge I was on was. I thought that it was normal to get out of jail only to be locked back up that night.

It wasn't abnormal for me to get pulled over and when I opened the car's door fifteen or twenty beer cans would fall out onto the pavement making a cling, cling, cling sound. The officer would say "Sir, have you been drinking?" and I would reply in my slurred voice "No". He would then say "Can you step out of the vehicle, sir?" and proceeded to give me a field sobriety test. He would ask me to stand on one foot and touch my nose, which I would say I couldn't do even if I hadn't been drinking. It always ended up with me going to jail.

I was okay as long as I wasn't locked up for long periods of time, because if I was I would start to withdraw from alcohol.

It is so weird to wake up, not remembering the events that took place the night before. I would open my eyes and I would have to look twice, and then I would see the bottom of the bunk above me. I would remember how it would look from the times I was incarcerated before and I would know immediately that I was in jail; that and the jump suit that would say Property Of "So And So" County, which I would have on.

I was in numerous jails through out the state of Florida, but the jail in downtown Miami was the one I disliked the most. There were about a hundred inmates, packed into a fifty person cell. The cell was only equipped with two toilettes that were in the middle of the room. The only thing that gave you any privacy was the sheets that were hung up to block the view.

I hated to go to the bathroom there because everyone could see you go. And if you were not big and intimidating, (which I was not), by the time you got back to the place where you slept the other inmates would have taken your pillows and anything else that you had managed to get for comfort.

The other jails that I was in were newer and were in better shape, but the jail in downtown Miami was old and crowded.

Needless to say I didn't like being incarcerated. But I was in jail enough times that you would think I did.

# Stage Forty Three Of My Life

### *My sixth suicide attempt*

Because of my circumstances and my clouded mind, from all of the drinking I was doing. I went into a deep depression and I slit my wrist.

I was living in Kendall with Ricardo at the time and had no insurance so I was taken to Lackson Hospital's psychiatric unit. I don't remember how they found out I had not insurance, but someone did find out this time.

They stitched up my wounds and released me. I was only in the hospital overnight. I was so out of it then. I promised Ricardo that I would never do that again.

After this attempt, I didn't need to try suicide anymore because I was drinking all of the time. I was in such a bad state that I didn't know reality from fantasy. If I didn't get help soon I would drink myself to death.

# Stage Forty Four Of My Life

### *Call from my brother*

Since my family in Kentucky didn't know how bad my drinking had become and how bad my previous drug use had been, my brothers thought it would be okay to have me to come up to help out my mother. She had been having symptoms of the beginning stages of Alzheimer's disease. (Alzheimer's disease is a horrible disease that attacks the mind the disease basically erases everything in your memory).

The first thing my brothers noticed that gave them a clue that my mom might have Alzheimer's disease was that she would believe everything she dreamed. She would forget small things like important dates and stuff. And she had to be reminded to eat and take her medicine. I went up there to help her out as much as I could; it turned out it was a blessing in disguise, because I needed help too.

# Stage Forty Five Of My Life

*Losing my ability to walk*

After I was there about a year I lost my ability to stand up or walk due to atrophy of the muscles. (Atrophy is caused by being inactive and the non use of muscles). All I would ever do was lay on my bed and drink; I never exercised.

The loss of the ability to walk was devastating. Many of the things that I took for granted were gone. Just getting up and going to the bathroom like a normal person was impossible.

Since I couldn't go to the bathroom I would have to use anything I could get as a toilet. I urinated, had bowel movements, and threw up in a waste basket.

Just like it was a natural occurrence to have to urinate when I woke up, it was also natural for me to have to vomit as soon as I opened my eyes. I would throw up three or four times a day. Sometimes when I had drunk too much and my stomach was full I would throw up just so that I could drink more.

I couldn't climb up on the bed so I had a mattress put on the floor. That is where I developed atrophy of the muscles and lost my ability to walk, due to the lack of exercise.

# Stage Forty Six Of My Life

### *Running out of vodka*

When I would run out of vodka I would start to panic. My body needed alcohol. First I would have to get my mom to go to the grocery store to get me a bottle of mouth wash, because I knew mouth wash had a high content of alcohol. I knew it would hold me over until I could get to the liquor store, and after drinking it, at least I could think straight.

Then I would have to figure out how I was going to get out to the truck for her to take me to the liquor store, which I knew would be complicated because of my atrophy.

The drive to Paducah (the nearest city with a liquor store) to get my alcohol was always stressful. My mom's Alzheimer's disease had progressed to the point that she couldn't remember how to get to a place where she had been to a million times. On top of the anxiety of getting the alcohol that my body desired and needed, I would have to tell her which way to turn and where.

Since the alcohol content in the mouth wash was so minimal, I was also worried that I would start having seizures before I got to the liquor store. I had gone into seizures in the past and it was common, that these were the first stage of the withdrawals I would go through every time I ran out of alcohol. I was buying vodka by the half gallon size, and sometimes I would drink two of those. In my mom's confused state I would tell her that we were going to get bottles of water and she would believe me.

# Stage Forty Seven Of My Life

### Drugs and Alcohol take a toll on my body

The alcohol was taking a toll on my body and on my mind. My liver had shrunken from the cirrhosis, so after drinking small amounts of alcohol, I would start seeing streaks of electricity on the wall, and then the streaks would turn into little people with wings, that I would call pixies. I know it sounds strange, but the streaks of electricity would turn into these humorous little people that were about six inches tall, who would eventually become mean.

The first part of my intoxication, I would be laughing, because the little people would be doing something funny. Then they would take flight and try to hit me in my head. Either I was laughing or I was trying to hit the pixies with a fly's swatter. Either way I know it looked crazy.

I would get so drunk, that I would dial the phone at random and talked to whoever answered. I was good at drunken dialing.

When I would wake up and look in the mirror and my hair was wild I would just drink until I thought it looked good again. The mind is a powerful thing, but when saturated with alcohol anything can be believable.

# Stage Forty Eight Of My Life

### My last suicide attempt

My moods would go from one extreme to the next. I was either very happy or very sad. One night I was so depressed that I went into a back room of the house got a gun that my mom had for protection; I put it to my temple and pulled the trigger. I was trying suicide again, I had thought that I would never try that again, but here I was.

I heard the hammer go click, but thank God my brother had removed the bullets that morning. I don't know if he suspected something, but I am glad he took them out, or my brains would have been blown all over the wall and I would not be here to tell my story.

# Stage Forty Nine Of My Life

### Almost dying

I was constantly being rushed to the hospital for alcohol and drug related reason. To date, the last time that I was taken to the hospital was when a vein burst in my esophagus and I almost bled to death.

It was 2001 and the last thing that I remember is becoming dizzy. I guess I had passed out because in the morning my mother's neighbor came in to check on my mom, and found me on the floor in a pool of blood. She called an ambulance, and I was rushed to the closest hospital.

The esophagus, (the part of the throat that goes from your mouth to your stomach) had been eaten away by the alcohol that I was consuming. I had this disease that made my veins weak, and since my liver was scarred and the blood didn't want to flow through it, the blood accumulated in my veins and the one in my esophagus burst. It expanded out like a balloon being filled with too much air and finally popped. I almost bled to death. When I was admitted to the hospital they gave me six blood transfusions, but they still could not get my blood pressure up.

The doctors told my family members, to call everyone and come to the hospital to say their good byes because they didn't think I was going to make it through the night. They thought I was going to die from having lost so much blood. I made it through that ordeal, but I did almost die.

I was diagnosed with cirrhosis, which is a disease of the liver, and I was diagnosed with the Hepatitis C virus, which is a disease of the blood that the doctors think I got from using dirty needles.

When the doctor asked me if I would get treatment for alcoholism, being the typical alcoholic I said that I didn't think I had a problem."

That is how this disease is, I was drinking everyday. Sometimes I would end up drinking a gallon of vodka. I had a vein burst in my esophagus, and I almost bled to death. I was in the emergency room a couple of times a month having the contents of my stomach pumped because I had drank too much, but I thought that alcohol was not a problem.

The doctor left the room; I think he was unable to conceive the thought that I didn't think I had a problem with alcohol. About an hour later, after the doctor told me that I should get treatment for alcoholism, the nurses disconnected my IVs; the sedatives they were giving me were starting to wear off, and I started to withdraw from alcohol once more.

# Stage Fifty Of My Life

*Getting off of alcohol and tranquilizers*

I knew something was wrong, but I didn't know what. I was going to withdraw whether I wanted to or not. I started having seizures, and I started to hallucinate.

At first the withdrawals weren't scary because I was hallucinating that my Mom, my uncle Ted, my aunt Millie and my cousins were there. I would be talking away and the nurse would come in and ask me who I was talking to. It must have looked weird to her because there was no one there.

My withdrawals continued to get worse and my hallucinations became scary. Instead of people I started seeing bugs! I thought the hospital sheets were infested with ants; there would be little mounds of ants all over. I would look down and I would yell; the nurse would come in, and ask me why I was yelling and I would say "because of the ants." She would say "There aren't any ants in here," and I would look down and all of the ants would disappear.

I also saw these big moths fly into the room and land on the curtain's rack. The bugs would land in a row, and I thought they looked as if they were lining up so that they could attack me. Later on I found out that the bugs were curtain rings that hung along the curtain track.

I would pull out the IVs that the nurses had put back in my arms to give me fluids. I thought they were snakes going into my veins. The doctors had my hands restrained so that I wouldn't pull the new IVs out. My ordeal was real, and I was beginning to have to face reality. Here I was, lying in a hospital bed with my hands tied, going through withdrawals from alcohol.

Never, in my wildest imagination, would I have dreamed that I would end up this way. The agony of withdrawing that I had always heard or read about was coming true.

I suffered from withdrawals from alcohol for about a week; they were intense and sometimes scary. I had gone through it all and now I was finally free from the grip that alcohol had on me. Or at least I thought so.

The doctors were slowly getting me off the tranquilizers at the same time, which wasn't an easy withdrawal either. I think coming off of the tranquilizers was one of the hardest things that I have ever had to do.

In the beginning of my experimentation I had always heard that tranquilizers were not addictive. But then I read that you could never get off the tranquilizers once you have become addicted to them; so for years, I always thought that I would have to take tranquilizers for the rest of my life.

I learned through experience that is not true. You can get off them; it may be hard but it is possible.

I had finally finished going through the horrible withdrawals from the drugs and alcohol, but I had forgotten that I couldn't walk. I got up to go to the bathroom like I had done in the past and I fell and landed face first on the hard floor. I busted my forehead open and it started to gush blood. I had to get six stitches done to close up the wound. After having all of the stitches that I had from slicing my wrist, this was a piece of cake.

After they took out the stitches the doctors didn't know what to do with me because I didn't have a job. I still couldn't walk, and my mom was going to my brother's house in Clarksville, TN. to live. I didn't have a place to go to, so the doctors - along with my family - had me put in a nursing home.

# Stage Fifty One Of My Life

### *The nursing home*

The nursing home that I went to was in Pembroke, Kentucky. I went from Paducah, Kentucky to Pembroke, Kentucky. It was a seventy mile long trip to get there; I was driven by taxi. The nursing home was in the middle of nowhere.

When I arrived at the nursing home, it had just started to snow. As we drove into the circular drive, up underneath the awning, I could see the glass doors that were the entrance to the building.

I was pushed inside the building in a wheelchair by a nurse; the first thing that I saw was a line of people sitting in their chairs in front of the television. I don't know if it was the medicine that they were given or just that time of the day, but half of the people there were asleep with their chins resting on their chests.

Most of the people there were elderly. There was one young girl, maybe in her twenties, who suffered from multiple sclerosis or something like that.

I was admitted and was taken to my room and introduced to my new roommate. The person whom I shared a room with was a seventy year old man who had been a good looking womanizer in his youth. But age had taken its toll. Now he was blind and had lung cancer. Even though he had numerous affairs through out his life his wife had always stuck by him. Now she was the only one that was there when visiting hours came.

I settled into the routine of the nursing home. For your daily shower, you would get on a plastic chair that looked like a toilet; it had wheels and could be maneuvered around easily. The nurse would spray you with a shower head. At first having someone give you a shower was humiliating but I got used to it.

We ate three times a day, but going to the dining room was always exciting. There was always something going on; either someone was yelling because they didn't want to eat or someone would start fighting because someone's wheelchair had bumped into their table. For people in their older years, they sometimes acted like they were infants.

For entertainment we would play games like Bingo or do arts and crafts. I was good at Bingo, but since I did have an advantage of being in my thirties playing against eighty year old invalids, I would lose on purpose. Or maybe I just didn't want to admit that I had been beaten by someone who was wheel chair bound and living in a nursing home." I couldn't walk, so my first order of business was to start my physical therapy. At first it was hard, but after I started to develop my muscles back it was easy.

For coordination we would pass a beach ball around, but I spent most of my time on the double bars practicing my walking.

The stay at the nursing home was weird; I went through the physical therapy, and I built my muscles up. But I still couldn't walk right. The doctor said that through the years of abusing drugs and alcohol I probably suffered some nerve damage.

I was so grateful to be able to walk. I was afraid that I would never walk again. To this day I choose to walk to a lot of the places that I could get a ride to, because I am so grateful that I actually enjoy it.

I was only thirty nine years old at the time. I was too young to be in a nursing home but I was too old to be acting like I was. I did a lot of thinking and decided it was time for me to get better and go home.

The nursing home wouldn't release me unless I had somewhere to go. I wanted to go back to Ricardo in Miami, but I didn't know how he would feel since he had put up with my drug addiction, my suicide attempts, and my alcoholism. I guess compared to all of the other stuff I had done this wasn't that bad, and at least now I was trying to get help for my problem.

# Stage Fifty Two Of My Life

## *Coming back to Miami*

Ricardo was glad that I was okay and wanted me to come back to Miami. So they released me on his word. My brother took me to the airport in Nashville and I flew back to Miami. I was glad to be back. Now I could start working on living the rest of my life.

After everything that I had been through, I thought all of my troubles were over. But they were just beginning. I had gone through withdraws, but now I had to stay sober. I had stopped drinking and taking drugs, but now I had to "stay stopped," and staying stopped is the hardest part.

I realized that this addiction was a disease which controlled the way I would think. When I think back about the days when I would relapse, I realize I would start thinking differently days before I would have my first drink or my first drug.

After I got back to Miami I was trying to do the right things. I know for a good life all you have to do is to make the right choices. I spent years making the wrong ones, but now I was going to only make the right ones.

I joined a chapter of Alcoholics Anonymous. ("A. A" is an organization of other people who drank or used drugs in the past and can help you by telling you what the decision to use alcohol or drugs caused them.) I had gone to meetings in the past, but I wasn't serious; this time I was. This time I was going to do everything in my power to stay sober. But I guess I made a wrong choice somewhere because I didn't.

# Stage Fifty Three Of My Life

### *Doing the right thing*

My brothers decided they were going to send my mom from Nashville to Miami to stay with me. I told them that it would be okay, not knowing that I wasn't ready to take on that much responsibility. I was doing the right things. I was going to A.A. I had gotten a sponsor, and I was attending meetings twice a day.

However, the thing about A.A. is that you really have to like to socialize and talk in front of large groups of people. At the A.A. meetings I attended, they would pass around a microphone to each person at the end of the meeting and give you a chance to say what was on your mind. You didn't have to talk, but I felt obligated to.

I do, however, fully recommend A.A. meetings. They help a lot of people, and not everyone is as shy as I am. (And I was also living a lie there, because I never told anyone there that I was gay, and it was a group for heterosexual people). I don't think anyone would have passed judgment; I just never said anything.

# Stage Fifty Four Of My Life

### *The relapse*

From all of the stress of feeling obligated to talk in the A.A.

meetings and after a few weeks of taking care of my mother (who was hallucinating at this point), I thought I was going to have a nervous breakdown. I decided to take a small shot glass of vodka for my nerves.

The next day I had to take a shot glass of vodka so that I would not get the shakes, and by the end of the week I was drinking large amounts of alcohol so that I would not have withdrawal symptoms.

It happened that fast; it only took one time, and it was like I had never stopped drinking. It was like the week in the hospital didn't matter. I went from being sober to being addicted again. I didn't know what to do because I didn't ever think I would be in that situation again. I continued to drink for the next couple of months, but there was no way that I could take care of my mom.

Ricardo called my oldest brother who still lived in Nashville and asked him what we should do. He said I should put my mom on a plane; he would arrange for someone to meet her half way and she could come back to Tennessee to be taken care of.

My other brother and his wife, who lived in Clarksville, Tennessee, took care of her for a while. When it became too much for them to handle, my brother had her placed into an assisted living home, where she remains today. I am writing this book in 2008 so I hope everything's the same by the time I get it published.

After my mom flew back to Tennessee I continued to drink and go to the A.A. meetings. I was still not telling the group that I was gay; I don't know why I just didn't. On my eighth month of supposedly being sober I got up to get my chip (the club gives out plastic chips for each month that you remain sober), but I was so drunk I tripped and fell in front of everyone. After I did that, I stopped going to A.A; because I was embarrassed of having fallen, and because I had started to drink heavily again.

The alcohol had taken over my life again. As soon as I woke up I would have to take a drink. I would buy half pint bottles instead of one big bottle, because they were easier to hide. After I had drunk some of the alcohol I would hide it because I knew I would need it when I woke up. But half of the time when I woke up I couldn't remember where I had hidden it.  I would tear the apartment up looking for my alcohol. If I couldn't find it I would have to buy a new bottle.

Since I didn't have any money, I would have to find spare change wherever I could. I hadn't looked for work since I had gotten back from the nursing home, because I was still trying to figure out what condition my body was in. (Because of the hepatitis C, I don't work to this day; it causes extreme fatigue). I don't suffer any symptoms from the cirrhosis except leg pain because the blood doesn't want to flow through my liver and backs up in my legs.

After I would find enough money, I would be happy. I would finally be able to get the liquid that my body craved. Because I was drinking a lot again, my brain didn't think right. What made logical sense then doesn't now. Instead of paying $2.95 for a half pint of vodka across the street, I would walk from 132$^{nd}$ Avenue to 107$^{th}$ Avenue so I would only have to pay $ 2.05 for a half pint. That's a long way to walk to save 90 cents.

# Stage Fifty Five Of My Life

### *Another chance*

Martha, my best friend (and also a friend of Ricardo) was scared. I was drinking large amounts of alcohol, and my behavior was out of control. I would get mad easily, and I would turn violent when I drank. Alcohol had never affected me this way before; usually it made me a happy person, but now it was doing the opposite. Ricardo and my friend had me arrested. They thought that a night in jail would do me good.

Nobody knew - not even me - that I had a bench warrant from 1996, and that after I was arrested that the jail would have no choice but to keep me locked up.

I was arrested and my sentence was for ninety days. I went to the jail in downtown Miami first. They fingerprinted me and took my picture.

I was then sent to Miami-Dade West; then I was sent to the Stockade and then I was sent to T.G.K. I stayed at each place a couple of hours, but T.G.K would be my home for the next two weeks. Then they expedited me to Lake County, where the bench warrant was from.

Before I was expedited they had me in a jail cell in Miami. I was withdrawing from alcohol again but I didn't tell anyone. I should have, but I didn't.

I didn't have any seizures like I was afraid I would. I was on anti-seizure medication the whole time. I had told the guards at the jail that I was prone to seizures, and they gave me the medication to keep me from having them.

It was a horrible experience though. I did have hallucinations and I would believe everything that I dreamed was true.

The hallucinations I was having were weird. Since my thoughts were so strange and since I didn't tell anyone that I was withdrawing from alcohol, the people who worked at the jail thought I was a crazy person and sent me to the psychiatric floor of the jail.

I would have probably liked the people there, but I had no idea were I was. I just thought they had placed me in a cell with a crazy person.

The guy I was in the cell with was very crazy. He would talk to himself. He would tell me he was going to kill me, and that there was no use in yelling because by the time the guards got there it would be too late for them to do anything. He would not let me eat, and he would make me give him all of my food. He would sit on top of the toilette so that I could not use it. I would wait until the guards took him to go take a shower (which was every other day) or for him to go to sleep and then I would go to the bathroom.

When I complained to the guards, they put me in a cell, with another crazy person who sang songs non stop. (Just the people that I was put into cells with was enough to make anyone crazy).

I was examined by a psychiatrist, who asked me a couple of questions, and then he told the guards that there was no reason for me to be there.

92

By now my withdrawals were gone and I was back to my old self again. I was transferred back to the regular jail. After I got back to the jail, I was transferred from the cell that was on the second floor to a cell that was on the first. I initially thought it was one of the first steps they took before I would be released, but I was wrong. It was just a holding cell until they came to expedite me to Lake County to serve my time there.

Lake County Jail was four hours north of Miami. I was taken up there in a transport van that the correction department used to transport prisoners. There were three of us in the van being transferred to different jails along the way.

We made stops at every jail so a four hour trip took six hours. It seemed like forever in the heat, because the back of the van was not air conditioned. I felt like I was being unfairly punished, the heat was so bad. When I got to the jail in Lake County, I went through the booking phase again. The guards took my clothes and gave me a jumpsuit to wear. Their jumpsuit was orange, and said: Property of Lake County Jail" on the back. After that they finger printed me and they took my picture again. I guess it is their policy to publish the pictures to the public, because you can now, to this day, access my mug shot on the internet.

I was put into a cell with four other guys; they were in jail for petty crimes, nothing serious. I passed the time reading. I also looked forward for Thursdays to come because that is the day commissary would come. (Commissary is the department that handles the snacks and necessities you could order each week). It would cost money, so the few inmates who were fortunate - like I was - to have someone send money, would place their orders on Monday to be delivered on Thursday.

I spent an hour a day walking around the perimeter of the jail. I spent the rest of my time with my nose in a book. You had to find a way to pass the time, because time seemed to go so slow when you are incarcerated.

I only ended up serving thirty days because Ricardo wrote to the judge and sent copies of the paperwork showing that I had complied with everything that had been asked of me the first time

I had been arrested and thus the bench warrant was an error. The judge ended up reducing my sentence.

# Stage Fifty Six Of My Life

### *Gaining and losing weight*

After I had survived the jail, I was clean and sober. But because of the anxiety, I ate a lot and gained a lot of weight. I went from 170 lbs. to 230 lbs. I didn't realize it at the time but I was getting big.

People who I hadn't seen in a while would tell me that I had gained weight. If it hadn't been for that, and the time I went to a restaurant to eat and barely fit into the booth, I wouldn't have realized how big I was getting.

I didn't know what to do; I had never had this kind of problem before. I had always been thin. I decided to join a gym. I started eating right, and I started exercising. I did cardio (which is doing anything that will get your heart rate up so that you lose weight). I would do sit ups, and I would use the different machines to work different muscles. Between eating right and exercising daily I lost over seventy four pounds.

Losing the weight was easy, but the hard part is keeping the weight off. It's like drinking and taking drugs; it's easy to stop but the hard part is staying stopped.

# Stage Fifty Seven Of My Life

### *Bettering my life*

Since I did get another chance, I've decided to better myself. I do not want to be on my deathbed and wish I had tried to do certain things like writing a book, learning to speak Spanish or what ever else I end up doing. I met the lady in my Spanish class who said I should write my story and is helping me with this book. I want to experience everything that I can. I've been through a lot but at least there's hope, and I never had hope before. Now I enjoy the simple things in life.

The doctors have decided that they are going to treat my Hepatitis C. The anticipation of starting the treatments excites me and scares me at the same time; I am excited at the thought of finally getting rid of the disease, but I am scared of the side effects of the medication.

My Hepatitis C couldn't be treated when I started to write this book because my platelet level was so low, now it has risen so they are going to go ahead and start the treatments.

There are a lot of side effects with the medication they use to treat the disease. I have always wanted to get rid of the virus so I will have the treatments. The treatments are supposed to last a year, but a year is such a short time. Getting rid of that virus will be another chapter in my life.


# Stage Fifty Eight Of My Life

*Surviving the drug and alcohol stage*


I lived through the drug and drinking stage of my life. Even though I have problems, I'm glad that I survived it and can talk about how life used to be. I am so lucky to be alive.

I don't know how I overcame my addiction. But when I was in Kentucky, Ricardo stuck by me and was very supportive. Every night he would call me and we would say the "Our Farther" prayer over the phone. With all of the positivity of the prayer and with

Ricardo's support I overcame the overwhelming odds that were against me.

I know of people who still use and they don't want to stop. They say that they have to die one day, but the problem is that you don't always die. Sometimes you have to go on living with the consequences of what you have inflicted on your body over the years. If there is one thing that I have learned it is that you can overcome the obstacles, no matter how dire they may seem.

# Stage Fifty Nine Of My Life

### *Staying sober*

I never drink or use drugs. I have tested my alcoholism once when my mom was here and I never want to do it again. I know it only takes one time and it is as if you have never quit. When I started my Spanish class I didn't know how much damage I had done to my brain. I didn't know if I would be able to memorize anything, or what my limitations were. I was lucky because the part of my brain that lets you remember stuff wasn't affected. I do consider myself very lucky because most people who led a life like I did either ended up dead, in jail, or institutionalized. But I made it, so maybe my story will help just one person from making the same mistakes that I made.

# IV
# EPILOGUE

Well, since writing this book, I've learned that I abused drugs and alcohol because I started to experiment because everyone else did. And I wanted to suppress my homosexual feelings. Through experimenting and using drugs and alcohol to suppress my feelings I became addicted.

Not much has changed; Denise is still in a nursing home in St. Petersburg, Florida.

Mark has gone back to school and has become a father; his fiancée is named Cassie and they plan to marry one day soon.

Samantha, who has changed her major so many times already, wants to go into business and is going to school at F.I.U. in Miami, Florida.

Sally is living in Orlando (also in Florida) with her oldest sister Carol and has one son, and is doing well. Maggie just moved back to Orlando. I still keep in touch with them; they are also survivors of this disease.

I haven't seen my friend Peter in years, and I am not sure what became of him.

I still live with Ricardo and we have been together for almost nineteen years.

I go to the gym everyday and I continue to eat right. There are no more suicide attempts.

I like to dream because my best friend Martha is still alive in my dreams. I keep myself busy with my hobbies and taking care of my granddaughter. My hobbies include making YouTube videos, painting, learning Spanish, and working on my blog.

You can access my YouTube channel at www.youtube.com/mikespalding. You can access my blog at www.kennethmichael.blogspot.com.

Life is finally good for me.

www.ingramcontent.com/pod-product-compliance
Lightning Source LLC
Chambersburg PA
CBHW031231280526
45784CB00004B/1533